m

A HORRID FA

HORRID HENRY'S
BUGS

Francesca Simon spent her
childhood on the beach in California, and
then went to Yale and Oxford Universities
to study medieval history and literature.
She now lives in London with her family.
She has written over fifty books and won the
Children's Book of the Year in 2008 at the
Galaxy British Book Awards for *Horrid Henry
and the Abominable Snowman*.

Tony Ross is one of Britain's
best-known illustrators, with many
picture books to his name as well as
line drawings for many fiction titles.
He lives in Wales.

For a complete list of
Horrid Henry titles, visit

www.horridhenry.co.uk

or

www.orionbooks.co.uk

A HORRID FACTBOOK
HORRID HENRY'S
BUGS

Francesca Simon

Illustrated by Tony Ross

Orion
Children's Books

First published in Great Britain in 2013
by Orion Children's Books
a division of the Orion Publishing Group Ltd
Orion House
5 Upper Saint Martin's Lane
London WC2H 9EA
An Hachette UK Company

1 3 5 7 9 10 8 6 4 2

Facts compiled by Sally Byford.

ISBN 978 1 4440 0632 2

A catalogue record for this book is available from the British Library.

Printed in Great Britain by
Clays Ltd, St Ives plc

www.orionbooks.co.uk

www.horridhenry.co.uk

CONTENTS

Hello from Henry

Hi gang!

Bugs! Creepy-crawly, sticky, sluggy, slimy, leggy, squashy, bouncy – I love them all. Who wouldn't want to hang out with a load of ugly, grubby bugs?

Did you know there are cannibal bugs, and poo-eating bugs, and mum-eating bugs, and blood-sucking bugs, and vomiting bugs and…no, no, it's too gross, you'll just have to read this book and find out what the tarantula wasp does… Yikes!!!!!!!!!

Henry

BUG
BASICS

Bugs have been around for **300 million years** – they were on Earth long before humans and even before the dinosaurs!

95% of all animals are bugs, and for every person in the world, there are **200 million** bugs.

I'd gladly exchange 200 million bugs for one Peter.

Scientists divide all the bugs up into **different families** to help them work out **who's who** in the bug world.

Most of the bugs in this book are from one great big bug family – the **arthropods** – which includes all sorts of different bugs from **scary spiders** and **beastly beetles** to **creepy-crawly cockroaches** and **foul flies**.

The word 'arthropod' means **jointed foot** and that's what all these bugs have – legs made of stiff little sections with bendy joints.

Arthropods have **inside-out bodies**. They don't have a skeleton like us – instead they have a hard shell on the outside, like a **suit of armour**, to protect the soft squishy bits inside.

The arthropod family is divided into smaller families – **insects**, **arachnids**, **myriapods** and **crustaceans**.

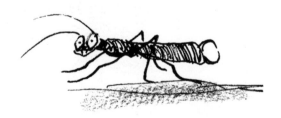

The **insect** family all have **six legs**, bodies made of **three parts** and two funny feelers on their heads. **Insects** can be beautiful like **butterflies** or ugly like **earwigs**.

The **arachnid** family all have **eight legs** and bodies made of two parts. **Spiders** are the most super-scary arachnids, but tiny **ticks** and miniscule **mites** are part of the family too.

The creepy-crawly **myriapod** family, have lots of little legs, like centipedes and millipedes.

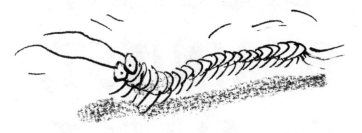

The **crustacean** family, like woodlice, have **14 legs**. Crabs and lobsters are crustaceans too, but they aren't bugs, because they live under the sea.

And some bugs don't have any legs at all, like soft-bodied **slugs** and **snails**, **wiggly worms** and blood-sucking **leeches**.

BIGGEST, BRAINIEST, SMALLEST, STRONGEST ...

Biggest – the gigantic owlet moth with a wingspan of 30 centimetres – as big as a pair of man's hands.

Heaviest – the African Goliath beetle, which weighs around 100 grams, about the same as an apple.

Smallest – the fairyfly is only 0.2 millimetres long – as small as a full stop in this book.

Longest – the giant
African earthworm
from South Africa is
nearly seven metres
long – longer than
three skipping ropes
tied together, but
only about as thick
as your finger.

**I'd love to drop
one of them on
Margaret's head.**

Strongest –
the Rhinoceros
beetle can lift
100 times its
own weight.
That's like
you lifting an
elephant!

Fastest flier – the horse-fly can fly at 145 kilometres per hour – faster than the top driving speed on the motorway in Britain.

Fastest runner – the American cockroach runs at a maximum speed of five km per hour. Human adults walk at that speed – but their legs are a lot longer.

Longest flight – the Painted Lady butterfly migrates all the way from North Africa to Iceland, a distance of nearly 6,500 km – which is the same as walking the length of a football pitch 65,000 times.

Highest jumper – a flea can jump 30 cm into the air, 130 times its height. That's like your dad jumping to the top of a skyscraper.

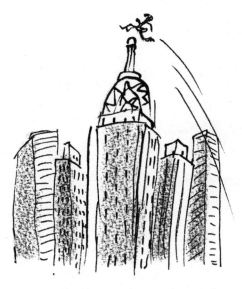

Coldest – the Kirby Carabid beetle lives in the Arctic and can survive temperatures of minus 51 °C. Brrrrr!

Hottest – the Cataglyphis ant lives in the Sahara Desert and can walk on sand as hot as 70 °C by moving its feet very quickly and using its long legs to keep its body off the scorching sand.

Most Venomous – just 0.006 milligrams of venom, like a tiny pinprick of blood, from the Brazilian wandering spider can kill a mouse.

Brainiest – a colony of ants has around the same number of brain cells as one human.

Biggest nest –

a wasp's nest 1.8 m by 1.5 m was found in the UK in 2010. It was 15 times bigger than a normal nest and contained half a million wasps!

Loudest – the cicada, which can sing as loudly as a road drill and can be heard half a kilometre away.

Bet it's not as loud as Margaret, though – you can hear her screams in Outer Space.

Largest spider's web – a web covering a 180 m area of trees and shrubs – the size of two football fields – was discovered in the US in 2009. Luckily, it was built by millions of small spiders, not one very big scary one.

Biggest Family – the queen termite lays 21 eggs a minute, and produces 30,000 eggs a day. If she lives for ten years, that's about 100 million children.

KILLER
BUGS

American killer bees look just like normal bees, but they will chase people for miles, attacking and killing, if they think their hive is in danger.

Army ants march at night in groups of up to one million, killing and eating bugs, birds, and even horses if they get in their way.

Yikes!

The **Australian black bulldog ant** bites and stings at the same time, squirting acid into the wound. Thirty bites from this little ant could **kill** a grown man.

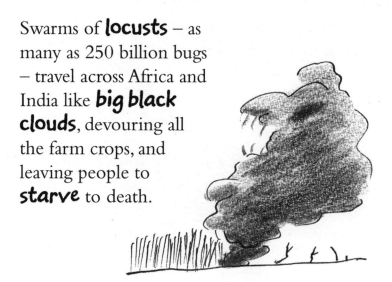

The **funnel-web spider is one of the world's deadliest spiders** – its venom has killed about 15 people in the last 100 years.

Swarms of **locusts** – as many as 250 billion bugs – travel across Africa and India like **big black clouds**, devouring all the farm crops, and leaving people to **starve** to death.

In hot countries, **mosquitoes** kill about **one million** people every year by stabbing their long pointy snouts into skin and spreading **disease**.

Six-eyed **sand spiders** hide in sand pits in the desert and leap out at their unsuspecting victims, injecting their **lethal venom**.

Hmm. Wonder if the local pet shop has one.

A bite from a **black widow spider** can make vulnerable people, like children or the elderly, very sick – and can sometimes kill.

WEIRD AND WONDERFUL

Crickets' ears aren't on their heads – they are on their stomachs or legs instead.

Many **bugs** breathe through **holes** in the sides of their bodies, which is why they drown in water.

When it's **cold** outside, bees stay inside their hives and **vibrate** their wings or **snuggle up** together to keep warm. Awww.

Bees have **five eyes**, but they still can't see the colour red – to them it just looks black.

The **praying mantis** is the only insect that can turn its head right round to look at you over its shoulder. **Scary.**

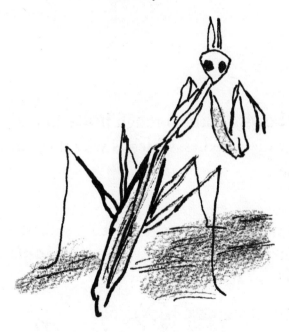

Insects usually shed their skins five to ten times in a lifetime, but **silverfish**, those slithery little bugs that lurk in **dark places** in your house, can do it up to sixty times.

Wasps can sleep – sometimes for **months** – while hanging by their teeth.

Snails never leave their **homes** – they are **born** with their shells already there and they stay firmly stuck to them until they die.

Maybe Peter will find a shell to crawl into one day.

Every time a **centipede** sheds its hard skin, it adds on yet another **pair of legs**.

Butterflies can **taste** with their **feet**! They can tell if a flower has nectar as soon as they land on it.

Mayflies spend most of their lives with their brothers and sisters in **mud** at the bottom of **lakes** and **rivers**. When they are fully grown, they all fly out at the same time, and live in the air for a very short time – sometimes for **only five minutes**.

Some butterflies have **tongues** as long as their bodies, but the **sphinx moth** beats them all, with a tongue that's three times as long as its body – more than 25cm in length.

SURVIVAL

Centipedes have jaws full of **venom**, which they use to stun and kill other bugs – and then eat them.

Wow! Who knew bugs were so horrid?

Spiders weave **webs** to catch other bugs for their **dinner**.

The **velvet ant** is really a **wasp**, but it looks so much like an ant that it can **sneak** into an ants' nest and attack.

Wouldn't that be a great way to attack the Secret Club?

The **spider wasp** lives in **tropical forests** and hunts giant tarantula spiders. It paralyses the spider with its sting, then feeds the spider flesh to its babies.

Venus flytraps are hairy meat-eating plants. When a bug touches the plant's hairs, the plant quickly closes, **trapping** the bug inside and poisoning it to death.

Butterflies and moths **scare off** attackers by flashing their brightly spotted wings.

Millipedes defend themselves by **curling** into a ball and pumping out a **poisonous gas**.

When **ladybirds** are frightened, they pretend to be **dead**.

But ladybirds are actually very **poisonous**, and if they are attacked, they bleed brightly-coloured and foul-tasting **blood** from their knees.

If a **snail** gets scared, it can **hide** inside its shell.

Worms are covered with **hundreds** of tiny bristles to help them **grip** as they wriggle along their tunnels. When a bird tries to tug a worm out of the ground, the worm clings on as hard as it can with its bristles.

Daddy longlegs are great at escaping! If you grab one by the leg, the leg just **breaks off** and the bug gets away. But sadly for the daddy longlegs, the leg never grows back.

Stink beetles put off predators by oozing out a liquid from their stomachs, which smells of **rotten cheese**.

Some bugs have brightly coloured bodies to warn their attackers that they **taste nasty** or have a sting.

With their **yellow-and-black stripes**, harmless **hoverflies** survive by pretending to be wasps.

BUG
GRUB

A **third** of all bugs are **meat-eaters** – most of them go **hunting** for their food, while a few feast on decaying meat or dung.

A **beehive** produces 22 kg of **honey** – that's about **50 jars** full – during the summer, which is the bees' food for the winter.

Wonder why they don't produce chocolate instead?

The **Bagheera kiplingi spider** from Central America is the only known **vegetarian spider** in the world – it likes munching on the tips of plants.

That's what Peter would be if he were a spider.

Some **spiders** make a **new web** every day. But they don't waste the old web – they roll it up into a ball and **eat it**.

Snails have something called a **radula** in their mouths, for grinding up their food. It's like a hard tongue covered in **thousands of tiny teeth**.

Spiders can't chew their food – they can only suck up liquids.

Spiders eat other bugs **alive!** They shoot poison from their **fangs** into a bug, which stops the bug from moving and turns its insides into mush. Then they slurp up the **sloppy glop**.

Yeah!

You **can't tell** if a bug has been eaten by a spider, because its hard outer shell is still there – only its **insides are missing**!

Most **snails** are vegetarians, but they're not fussy eaters – sometimes they make do with **soggy cardboard**.

Bird-eating spiders as big as a **dinner plates** have enormous appetites. They gobble up frogs, lizards and mice, as well as birds.

While female **mosquitoes** feast on **blood**, the males enjoy nectar from plants instead.

Dragonflies like **fast food**! They hold their prey with their legs and eat while they are flying.

Gobble on the GO.

Ants have **two stomachs**. One stomach carries its own food while the other carries food to share later with other ants.

One type of **woodlouse** makes itself at home inside a yellow ants' nest and then munches on the **ants' poo**.

Cockroaches love eating the **glue** on envelopes and on the back of postage stamps.

But **cockroaches** aren't fussy about their food – they'll eat anything! If they're really hungry, they'll even eat each other. **Bleccch!**

Wolf spiders eat each other. The females eat the males. The males eat older females. And the babies munch up their own mum!

That would be a scary house to live in.

GROSS-OUT!

The **burying beetle** buries the bodies of **dead birds** and lays its eggs close by. When the babies are born, mum eats a bit of the dead bird's flesh, pukes it back up and feeds it to her babies. Bleccch!

Slugs slither along on a layer of **slime** produced by their own feet.

A new type of **monster slug** from Spain, 12cm long, has been found eating **dead mice** and **dog poo**. These slugs create so much slime on the roads that they are a danger to drivers.

If your pillow is over two years old, a tenth of its stuffing is made up of dead **mites** and their poo.

If you see something that looks like black pepper all over your house, it could be **cockroach** droppings. Cockroaches poo on everything they eat and then spread it everywhere.

Cockroaches can produce **two million** horrible cockroach children in just one year.

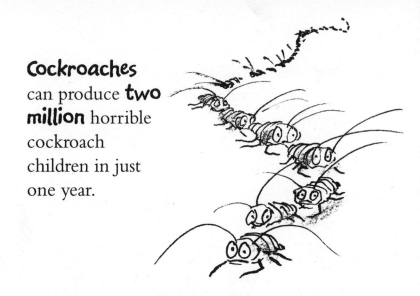

Horrible **houseflies vomit** on their food before eating it. Gross!

Doctors used to put **maggots** (baby flies) on wounds to eat the **dead flesh** and kill germs.

The **tarantula wasp** stings and paralyses a tarantula spider, then lays an egg on the spider's body. When the wasp baby is born, it makes a hole in the spider, slips inside and **eats the spider alive**.

A **mango fly egg** can burrow into your skin in just 25 seconds. A big spot will appear on your skin, with a little hole for the maggot to breathe through, and after a few days, you'll be able to see the black head of a maggot growing **inside you**. Watch out for these if you ever go to Africa!

The **queen ant** feeds her eggs with her own spit.

When **Australian social spider** babies are born, they suck their mum's blood until she's too weak to move. Then they **vomit** all over her, mush her up – and eat her.

BUG
MYTHBUSTERS

You can tell a ladybird's age by counting its spots.

MYTH! The number of spots shows what sort of ladybird it is, not its age. The most common British ladybirds are the two-spot ladybird and the seven-spot ladybird.

Spiders climb up the plug hole into your bath.

MYTH! They drop down from the ceiling and then get stuck because the walls of the bath are too slippery for them to climb out again.

If you chop a worm in half, a new worm grows from each piece.

MYTH! If you cut close to the end of the tail, the worm will regrow a new tail, but if you cut anywhere else, the worm will die.

If a money spider runs over you, you'll become rich.

MYTH! Long ago, people believed that if a money spider visited you, it had come to spin you new clothes and make you richer, but it's just an old superstition.

Earwigs crawl into your brain through your ear and make you go mad.

MYTH! They could crawl into your ear if they really wanted to, but they can't get any further because your eardrum is in the way.

Head lice only like dirty hair.

MYTH! They like dirty hair, clean hair, blonde hair, brown, red, black hair – any hair!

All spiders catch their prey in webs.

MYTH! Only about half of the different types of spiders catch food in their webs. The rest go out hunting, or sit and wait for food to come to them.

Spiders can lay their eggs under human skin. The skin swells up until finally hundreds of baby spiders emerge.

MYTH! The venom the spider leaves in your skin definitely can't turn into eggs or into baby spiders. Phew!

Bees gather honey from flowers.

MYTH! Bees gather nectar from flowers and take it back to their hive, where they turn it into honey.

Tarantulas are deadly to humans.

MYTH! Tarantulas are big, horrible, hairy and scary, but it's very unlikely one would bite a human. And even if it did, the venom wouldn't be strong enough to kill you.

Don't think I'll try this out myself, though.

If you find a spider in your house, it's kind to put them back outside.

MYTH! The spiders in your house are usually house spiders and have never been outside. Most of the time they remain hidden, but in August and September, male spiders wander around looking for female spiders. If you put them outside, they'll probably die.

Butterflies only live for a day.

MYTH! Some butterflies only live for three or four days, but most live for around 30 days and some live as long as ten months.

BLOODTHIRSTY
BUGS

Lazy **lice** don't bother to build their own homes – instead they live on other animals and suck their blood.

Leeches lurk at the bottom of ponds and canals, waiting to **suck your blood**. They have suckers at the front *and* back of their bodies – so there's no escape!

If you **swallowed** a leech, it would attach itself to the inside of your mouth or throat and suck your blood.

Leeches can **swell up** to three times their original size when they're feeding.

The tsetse fly **loves blood** so much that it will even bite through a **rhinoceros'** thick hide in its search for food.

Mosquitoes don't sting you – they **puncture** the surface of your skin and drink your blood.

Head lice can **change** their body colour to match your hair colour – the perfect way to **hide** on your head!

Bed bugs are a bit like **vampires** – they suck blood at night and hide away from the sunlight.

When they're stuffed full of blood, **bed bugs'** flat little bodies bloat up like **tiny balloons** and go red.

Ticks live on animals and suck their blood, sometimes expanding ten times in size after a huge meal.

NIFTY NICKNAMES

The name **centipede** means **'hundred legs'**.
But weirdly, lots of centipedes only have 30
legs…

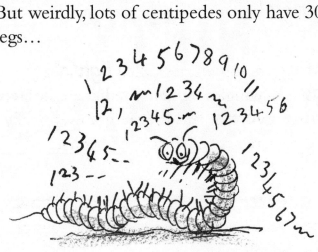

…And **millipede** means **'thousand legs'**,
although they actually only have between 40
to 200 pairs of legs. The scientists who named
these bugs couldn't count!

Crane flies are better known as **'daddy longlegs'** because of their long spindly legs.

Fireflies are sometimes called **lightning bugs**, and wingless female fireflies are known as **glow-worms**. But they're not even really flies – they're actually a type of beetle.

Giant water bugs are also known as **'toe biters'** because they like to bite the toes of people paddling in the water.

Water boatmen have powerful, hairy legs which they use to row themselves through the water.

Water striders are called **pond skaters** because they walk on water with their long legs.

The **whirligig beetle** whirls around and around very fast on the water surface. Its eyes are divided into two halves, so that it can see above and below the water surface at the same time.

Dung beetles are so called because they love eating manure. Mmmm!

Shield bugs are known as **stinkbugs** because the parent bug produces a powerful smell to protect her eggs and young babies from attack.

Imagine having your own built-in stinkbomb!

Butterflies got their name because they flutter around while milk is being churned to butter.

SPOOKY
SPIDERS

Half of all women and a **fifth** of all men are terrified of spiders. What a bunch of scaredy pants!

All spiders have eight horribly **hairy legs**, and all eight legs have six **knobbly knees** and two little **claws** at the end – a grand total of **16** claws and **48** knees.

The spider with the longest legs is the **giant huntsman spider**. With its 15cm-long legs, it's as big as the head of a **tennis racquet**.

Spiders' webs are made from liquid silk **inside** the spider's body. When the spider pulls the silk out with its legs, it **hardens** into thread.

Tarantulas' **hairy stomachs** are their secret **weapon**. The hairs are very **sharp**, and if a tarantula is threatened, it rubs the hairs with its legs and shoots them at its attacker.

Watch out for the fierce **funnel-web spider** from Australia. Its fangs are so strong, they can bite right through a human fingernail.

The **trap-door spider** lives in an underground burrow with a disguised web **trap-door**. When a passing bug touches the web, the trap-door springs open, the spider grabs it – and **dinner** is served …

The **bolas spider** fishes for food. It swings out a line of silk with a **sticky glob** on the end, until it sticks to the body or wings of its favourite food.

The male **nursery web spider** wraps up a tasty bug in silk and gives it to the female as a **present**.

The **brown recluse spider** is shy and lives alone – but if you frighten one, it'll give you a very **nasty bite**!

The **spitting spider** spits out its gluey silk at a bug's legs or wings. The bug gets all tangled up in the silk ... and the spitting spider moves in for **the kill**.

SUPER SENSES

Ants talk to each other by touching **feelers**, and they listen to sounds through their legs.

Bees don't buzz with their mouths. They make the buzzing sound by flapping their **wings** very fast – up to **200** times a second.

Flies can find **sugar** with their **feet** – which are **ten million times** more sensitive than a human tongue.

Just think if I could find hidden sweets like that. Wow.

Male **crickets** make that **chirping** noise you hear on hot summer days by scraping their back legs against their front wings or rubbing their two front wings together. The females don't make any noise at all!

Even though they can have up to eight eyes, most **spiders** have very **bad eyesight**. They have to feel their way around with their **body hair**.

But **hunting spiders** have brilliant eyesight. They can spot their prey at long distances – and scuttle in for the kill.

The male **Indian moon moth** is a super sniffer – he can smell a female moth over five km away.

Honeybees talk to each other – by **dancing**! A scientist has even worked out what the different dance moves mean. A bee returning with food from flowers nearby dances round in a little circle, while one returning from further away dances in a figure-of-eight while wagging its tail. Weird.

Butterflies smell through their **feet** – they can land on a flower and instantly know that its nectar will be good to eat.

Even if they are underground, **worms** can sense when it's **raining**.

When an **ant** finds food, it leaves a trail of scent for the rest of its family to follow.

UGLY
BUGS

Weird-looking **diopsid flies** found in South-East Asia and Southern Africa can spy around corners because their eyes stick out on **long stalks**.

The **thorn bug**, a type of treehopper from Central America, has a helmet on its back which looks just like a tree thorn.

Most flies have **ugly mugs**, but the **robber fly** from North America is even uglier, with a thick bristly **beard** on its face.

Wait till they see Peter - he'd win their ugly prize hands down.

Stomach-turning **tarantulas** are the biggest, hairiest and scariest of spiders.

Comma caterpillars aren't pretty – they look like pieces of **bird poo**.

The milky-white **flatworm** is almost see-through – you can see what it's been eating. Urrrgh!

If you think garden snails are ugly, imagine the **largest snail in the world** slithering along on its silvery slime – the **African giant snail** – which is the size of a man's hand.

The **giraffe weevil** from Madagascar is one very weird weevil, with a long thin neck that's the same length as the rest of its body.

Stag beetles have big black jagged **jaws** that look like deer's antlers.

The **puss moth caterpillar** can pull a face like a **cross old cat.** But don't look too closely – it also spits out its half-eaten dinner mixed with acid.

WATCH OUT!
BUGS
ABOUT!

There are **millions** of **dust mites** living in your house, feasting on your **dead skin**. Bleccch!

Some **caterpillars** have **stinging hairs** containing **poisons**, which can hurt you if you touch them.

Slugs can **stretch** their bodies so that they are very long and thin, and then fit themselves into **tiny** spaces.

You can't keep **cockroaches** out! They can flatten themselves to the thinness of a piece of paper and slide into **tiny cracks** in the wall.

Bees only sting to defend themselves. Their stings **hook** into their victims and are left behind – and when the bee flies away, it dies.

Great defence . . . NOT!

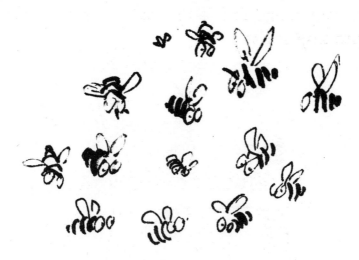

But **wasps** have **smooth stings**, which they can pull out of their victims in order to attack and sting again and again.

Flies are **filthy**! Before they land on your food, they've probably been stepping in a big smelly cowpat or stinky **dog poo**!

Tiny transparent **mites** live on human eyelashes and feast on dead skin and oil.

Don't look up! Some **slugs** can let themselves dangle down from a height on a **string of slime**. Yuck!

The **confused flour beetle** lays its sticky eggs in flour, which could end up in your cakes and pies.

The **wart-biter cricket** has such a powerful bite that it was used long ago in Sweden to gnaw off warts – ouch!

Scientists have estimated that that there are **two billion spiders** scuttling about England and Wales – that's around 500 in every square metre of grass.

In 2001, an Australian man went to an outside toilet and trapped a **red-back spider** in his jeans. He was bitten on the bottom more than **20** times!

STRANGE
BUT
TRUE ...

The body of a **cockroach** can live for nine days after its **head** has been **chopped off.** That's because its brain is actually in its body.

Some **moths** feed on the **tears** of deer, antelopes, crocodiles – and even sleeping birds. Watch out, Weepy William!

South American fire ants are **unstoppable** because they know how to work together as a **team**. If they have to get across water, they interlock their bodies to create a kind of **raft**.

In Malaysia, there are people who keep **jungle nymph stick insects** as pets and use their **poo** to make tea.

Stick insects don't panic if they lose a leg — they just grow a new one!

Snails are **hermaphrodites** — which means that every snail is both male and female at the same time.

Snoozy snails can sleep for **three years** at a time.

Don't tell Lazy Linda, it'll give her ideas.

Wood beetles make their homes in wood and they sometimes stay there even when it's chopped down and made into **furniture**.

Baby caterpillars are tiny when they are born, but they quickly grow **2,000 times bigger**! If a human baby grew at this rate, in a month it would weigh as much as **an elephant**.

Flies can walk **upside down** on your ceiling. Their feet have pads on them, covered with tiny, hooked hairs for **clinging** to surfaces.

Spiders use their silk to swing from place to place, just like Spiderman.

In July 1999, four **ladybirds** were **sent into space** on NASA's Columbia space shuttle, along with some greenfly, their favourite food, to see if they could still catch the greenfly in space. They did!

Bee bearding is a crazy competition to get the most bees on your face. Competitors put a queen bee in a small cage and wear it under their chin, as other bees swarm to a queen.

The biggest bee beard ever was **350,000 bees** in 1998 in the USA.

I don't care what the prize is - that's one competition I won't be entering for sure.

Bye!

the
orion star

Sign up for **the orion star** newsletter
for all the latest children's book news,
plus activity sheets, exclusive competitions,
author interviews, pre-publication extracts
and more.

www.orionbooks.co.uk/newsletters

Follow @the_orionstar on .